Th

Ches

Guide

England's Walled City, Shopping on the Medieval Rows, Roman Remains, Attractions, Walls Walk, History, Museums, River Dee, Cathedral, Access

TEXT, LINE DRAWINGS & PUBLICATION BY

GORDON EMERY ©2003 REVISED ©2018

www.gordonemery.co.uk

STONES (& TIMBERS) OF CHESTER BY

JAY HURST ©2017

PRINTED BY

Catford Print Centre, London SE6 2PN
www.catfordprint.co.uk

***Engraving from the Illustrated London News 16th October 1869:
"new townhall opened by the Prince of Wales'.***

After the old Town Hall and Exchange burnt down, a new one was built and opened, despite strikes and the contractor's death, in 1869. It contained a police station complete with cells in the basement, magistrates court and council chambers.

CONTENTS

Directory

Features

CHESTER: CITY, TIED TO TIME,
Founded by the Romans in AD79

'Deva' they called it a fortress and port
Surrounded by walls, from sandstone wrought.
For 300 years they made it their home
Then packed up their bags and went back to Rome.

The daughter of Alfred, Ethelfleda by name,
Re-established the fortress to combat the Danes.
She had a wall extension built down to the river
To protect from attacks the Welsh and Vikings would deliver.

The relics of St Werburgh arrived here as well
With miraculous powers, tradition does tell.
A shrine was established,
A pilgrimage place.
Encouraging peaceful visitors to come through the gates.

It's 1066 and, out of the blue,
William the Conqueror came conquering through.
He built up a castle that was strong and true,
And gave it to his nephew whose name was Hugh.
"Thanks, Uncle Bill", said Hugh the Wolf,
"I'll establish a monastery to fill the spiritual gulf".

In 1300, Edward was king,
A Charter was granted (it was the 'in' thing).
Proclaimed a city, prosperity unstopping.
They created the Rows for weatherfree shopping.
With plays on the streets for shoppers to see,
its success in business was no mystery.

However, success is a transitory thing;
Beware the pendulum on its back swing.
For fire and plague tore at its soul,
And a Civil War siege took a great toll.

Yet, here come the Victorians with a plan to put things right.
They've a scheme in mind for Chester and its clear in black and white.
Rebuilding and restoring, with a nod to history,
They didn't do such a bad job, the evidence you can see.

Chester: city, tied to time,
Past, present, future all intertwined.
The links are visible, no need to unlock,
Victorian hands touch Roman numerals
On the Eastgate Clock

DANNY MORRELL ©2002

INFORMATION POINTS

Visitor Information, Town Hall, Norhgate Street
Open 7 days
Closed Christmas, Boxing Day, New Year's Day
01244 405340
visitchester.com
email: welcome@chestervic.co.uk

Grosvenor Shopping Centre
01244 342942

Traveline 8am-8pm
traveline.info
0871 200 2233

Shopmobility (wheelchair & scooter hire) Frodsham Street Car
Park (opposite Tesco) 9.30-4.30 Mon-Sat 10.30 – 3.30 Sun
dialwestcheshire.org.uk
email: shopmobility@dialwestcheshire,org.uk   01244 312626

The Chester Grosvenor JH

ACCOMMODATION

Visitor Information has a call-in, telephone or web-based accommodation booking service. Choose from five star hotels to budget accommodation, comfortable bed and breakfast, self catering or country houses.

If you arrive in the city after the information office closes look for details at the train station or on the stands outside Visitor Information. There are three large city centre hotels (Chester Grosvenor, Eastgate Street; Macdonald New Blossoms, Foregate Street and Crowne Plaza, Trinity Street). There are also many other smaller hotels and pubs with accommodation such as The Pied Bull, Bull and Stirrup, and The Coach, all in Northgate Street. A concentration of small hotels can be found around the train station and on Hoole Road. Two budget hotels can be found down Watergate Street.

Cafe at The Northgate JH

EATING OUT

Chester has an enormous range of cafes, restaurants and take-aways: American, bar food, Belgian, British, Chinese, French, Greek, Italian, Indian, Japanese, Mediterranean, Mexican, Polish, Spanish, Thai, Turkish and Vegetarian/Vegan.

Although many eateries have vegetarian and vegan dishes, at the time of writing the only dedicated vegetarian/vegan bistro is Chai Station in Brook Street.

Some eating places are situated in Eastgate Street, Bridge Street, Lower Bridge Street and Pepper Street also in Watergate Street and City Road. There is a high concentration of take-aways and ethnic cafes and shops in Brook Street. A food and drink guide is available from Visitor Information.

HISTORICAL PLAQUES

Look out for Chester's blue plaques on buildings, ('Chester Inside Out' has walks covering most of them.) There are 40 multi-coloured millennium plaques on the pavement for the city's best buildings in the Millennium Trail (follow the little white on red arrows in the pavement). There are historical information boards on the walls and canal.

GUIDED TOURS AND BOAT TRIPS

The best way to see the city is by foot. This guide has a complete City Walls circuit, while the book 'Chester Inside Out' has four detailed walks from the Cross and a street by street index.

There are several guided walking tours run from Visitor Information (times vary). City guides for groups, different languages or special tours can also be contacted through them.

Chester Cathedral Tower Tours take place in the Cathedral
01244 500959   chestercathedral.com
There are pleasure boat cruises and small boats for hire on the River Dee.   01244 377955   chesterboat.co.uk
A restaurant cruise on the canal starts at the Mill Hotel
01244 350035 millhotel.com/lunch-dinner-cruises

ENTERTAINMENT

Jazz, blues, comedy, folk music, choral, organ recitals, lunchtime concerts, buskers, poetry readings, dance, historical talks and videos, exhibitions, sport, coach tours – all can be found in Chester – dates and times vary so get a current what's on guide from Visitor Information or Storyhouse.

Storyhouse, Northgate Street: theatre, cinema, cafe, restaurant and library.   storyhouse.com
Alexanders Live, Rufus Court, Northgate Street
                              alexanderslive.com   01244 401402
Telfords Warehouse, Raymond Street
                    telfordswarehousechester.com   01244 390090
The Live Rooms, Brook Street theliverooms.com   01244 318906
Mecca Bingo, Brook Street   01244 327165
Brewsters Fun Factory, The Twirl of Hay, Caldy Valley Road
CH3 5PR (a mile away)   01244 315766

The Boathouse JH

8

EVENTS

Many of Chester's festivals last a week so book accommodation in advance to coincide with some of the city's cultural events, from medieval to modern. Yearly dates from Visitor Information.

Film festival, Fringe festival, Folk festival (Kelsall), theatre, Midsummer Watch, Mystery Plays every five years, Christmas Lantern Parades & Winter Watch, Saturnalia, Open air theatre, Horseracing at England's oldest racecourse, Diwali, Chinese New Year, Music festivals, Raft Race, Chester Regatta – the world's oldest rowing races, exhibitions, fairs, conferences.

GOLF CLUBS

Chester Golf Club, Curzon Park	01244 677760
Westminster Park Golf Course, Hough Green	01244 680231
Upton by Chester Golf Club	01244 381183
Eaton Golf Club, Waverton	01244 335885

HEALTH AND FITNESS

A gym and a sports hall can be found at the Northgate Arena for reasonable prices.   brioleisure.org/centres/northgate-arena
01244 380444
Half a mile from the city on Liverpool Road, Total Fitness has 3 pools and two floors of gym equipment. Daily rate.
totalfitness.co.uk/clubs/chester   01244 393000

Clip 'n' Climb, 60 minutes of climbing experience. Unit 1A, Chester Gates Business Park, Chester, CH1 6LT
Clipnclimbchester.co.uk   01244 956780

POST OFFICES

Many shops sell stamps while there are post boxes all over the city but for specialist advice and parcels you may need a post office. The main one is in St John Street. There are also smaller ones in Northgate Street and Brook Street.

TAXIS

Find taxis at the Railway Station, the bus station and beyond the Eastgate Clock in Foregate Street. Private Hire offices in the city centre can be found in Bridge Street and Foregate Street. As a customer most pubs and restaurants will order your vehicle for you. All Chester hackney cabs and private hire cars have a council licence plate (white or yellow) with a number, while all drivers have an identity badge.
Hackney cabs should stop on request. Private Hire needs to be pre-booked by telephone or at their offices.
Largest Companies are:

Abbey Taxis	01244 318318
Chester Radio Taxis	01244 372372
Chester Taxicall	01244 458458
Chester Taxi Services	01244 421024
Empire Taxis	01244 421066
KingKabs	01244 343434
Taxi Chester	01244 794042

EMERGENCY

For emergency only (please do not put additional burdens on our public services)   freecall 999 to connect to ambulance, fire or police.

NON EMERGENCY

Police   freecall 101

Doctors and pharmacies
                    freephone 0800 132996
NHS 111   freecall 111
Casualty, Countess of Chester Hospital, Liverpool Road 01244 365224

Commercial Newsrooms JH

TOILETS

Most restaurants and cafes have toilets for their customers. There are public toilets at the Grosvenor Shopping Centre, Frodsham Street Car Park, Little Roodee Car Park, The Riverside Groves, the Cathedral, the Grosvenor Museum, Grosvenor Park, Storyhouse and the bus and train stations.

INTERNET

Free computer use available at Storyhouse. Northgate Street.
Internet cafes: Brown Sugar, 19 Handbridge   01244 683386
Cafe Chester, 20-22 Faulkner Street, Hoole   01244 344334

MUSEUMS and EXHIBITIONS

Grosvenor Museum, 27 Grosvenor Street   01244 402008
grosvenormuseum.westcheshiremuseums.co.uk
Admission is free 10.30 – 5.00 Mon – Sat, 2.00 - 5.00 Sun Donations welcome. Leave at least an hour to look around.

Roman soldiers en masse, impressive views outside the Roman fortress and the superb Roman stone collection: as if this wasn't enough there are temporary exhibitions, Stuart, Georgian and Victorian rooms, and a staff willing to answer questions.

Upstairs you can explore Chester's history through art, see Chester silver or visit Natural History Cheshire with varied exhibits from Seashore, River Dee, Delamere Forest, and Garden. The Mayor's Parlour, a panelled room with seats, was transferred here from a drinking club that boasted its own 'spoof' mayor and officials. *See History.*

Gravestone of a Roman 'optio' GE

Dewa (DEVA) Roman Experience, Pierpoint Lane off Bridge Street.
dewaromanexperience.co.uk   01244 343407
Admission charge 9.00 – 5.00 daily

Great news! You will find that your entrance fee will take you to Roman Chester (DEVA) by sea. The bad news is that you are to be transported in the bowels of a slave ship. However, you are free on arrival and can wander through a Roman market and check out the baths, before you travel back to the present where you can become an archaeologist and take a look underground at the layers of history laid down in the city bedrock. Artefacts are on display. There is a hands on room where you can be fitted up as a Roman soldier or just handle pottery and smell the aromas.

Cheshire Military Museum, The Castle
cheshiremilitarymuseum.co.uk   01244 327617
Admission charge 10.00 – 5.00 daily

The soldiers of Cheshire and their proud heritage, interactive displays for all the family.

Castle *Free Admission 10.30 – 3.30 daily except Mons 1.00 – 3.00 Sun*

Water Tower Exhibition *The northwest corner of the Walls*   *Admission charge*

St Michael's Church – Chester Heritage Exhibition, *Bridge Street*   *Admission charge*

Church of St John the Baptist Chester's Saxon Minster and original Norman Cathedral.
parishofchester.com   *Donations welcome*

The sword of Chester's first Norman earl. British Museum

Chester Cathedral The former Abbey of St Werburgh *chestercathedral.com 01244 324756*
    Donations welcome

PARKS AND OPEN SPACES

Chester's premier park to the east of the amphitheatre, colourful gardens, trees both interesting and gothically pollarded, play equipment, white Sicilian marble statue by Thorneycroft of second Marquis of Westminster – benefactor of park in 1867, arch from St Mary's Nunnery, old shipgate, arch from St Michael's Church, lodge with statuettes of Chester's Norman earls, miniature train (summer & some weekends and holidays only), duckpond, tame and hungry grey squirrels feed on monkey nuts – buy some before you visit, riverside views, carvings, representation of Ymir (Norse mythology), cafe, Billy Hobby's (wishing) Well covered by John Douglas' spired folly.

Edgar's Field, Handbridge   Riverside park supposedly where Edgar set off up river (see History), unique Roman carving of the goddess Minerva, riverside walk past the unusually named house 'Nowhere' – there's nowhere like it anywhere else! Views of Grosvenor Bridge downstream & Overleigh Cemetery (see below), graffiti of boats and lorries carved in park walls by fishermen's children while they waited for the boats to come home.

The Meadows   Cross the suspension bridge over the River Dee and you can wander upstream for miles on the riverside path. The Meadows were given to the people of Chester by a former mayor.

Overleigh Cemetery just downstream from Edgar's Field, or approach by crossing the Grosvenor Bridge. Not a park but, if you don't mind the company, beautiful trees and interesting gravestones including Mary Jonas – proud mother of 33 children died at age 85; Edward Langtree – husband of 'Jersey Lilly' mistress of Edward VII; and Mr and Mrs Christmas.

Roman Gardens, Newgate   Roman artefacts, walls.

Water Tower Gardens NW corner of the Walls   Play equipment, view of Walls and Water Tower.

Northgate Locks   Canalside parks, read or sit on the grass and watch the boats go by. You can follow the towpath north 10 miles on the flat to reach the National Waterways Museum, or east into the Cheshire countryside.

The Cop, Sealand Road   Skateboard park, views downriver, mudflats, birds, graffiti on WWII bunker.

Alexandra Park, Hoole   Bowls, tennis courts, play equipment, sculptures, playing field.

Sandy Lane, Boughton   Riverside park, views of Meadows.

Westminster Park, Hough Green   All year round 9 hole golf course, outdoor gym open space, BMX track, cricket, running track, putting, play equipment, tennis bowls, snack bar, parking. 01244 680231

Northgate Village Park behind Northgate Arena   Open space, ponds, access to greenway route 5.

Gamul Place   Tiny hidden park in the centre of the city.

Duke's Drive   Cross the Grosvenor Bridge and go around the first roundabout to enter through large iron gates. The driveway now stops at the bypass and no longer goes to Eaton Hall.

Caldy Valley Nature Park   A pleasant valley with sculptures starting from Sandy Lane, Boughton, a mile away.

Countess of Chester Country Park   A mile away on Countess Way, Parkgate Road.

St Michael's Arch in Grosvenor Park   GE

14

Cornice of Roman Wall rebuilt off Water Tower Street JH

CHESTER WALLS

The original walls at Chester were made of turf built in about 75AD by the Roman II Legion at their fortress DEVA. In around 102AD the XX Legion rebuilt the fortress walls in stone. The best remaining section of Roman wall under No 1 City Walls can best be seen as a slightly bulging 13 courses of sandstone masonry looking east and upwards from the Northgate Bridge.

Centurial Stone: '[Built by] the century of Ocratius Maximus, first cohort'

The walls were repaired again by the XX Legion a century or so later. The soldiers used old gravestones in its reconstruction. Up to 150 inscriptions, tombstones and sculptures were found built into the North Wall during the 19th century. Many are displayed at the award-winning Graham Webster Gallery at the Grosvenor Museum. Originally, they were painted in bright colours and would have lined the roads leading to the fortress.

In the tenth century, under Anglo-Saxon rule, Alfred's daughter Queen Ethelfleda probably extended the north wall to the river in the west, and the west wall to the river in the south, creating a walled town or 'burh' with a protected area four times the size of the former Roman fort. The remaining Roman fort walls on the south and west were removed or left to collapse. In Saxon and Norman times the walls were repaired by 'murengers' sent by the manorial lords of Cheshire. Walls and gates were built alongside the river by 1120.

The walls were fortified again in the Civil War to protect King Charles I's supporters inside the city against the Parliamentary forces attacking. Chester was the last city to hold out for the king, its citizens suffering hardship and starvation before surrendering.

King Charles Tower

In Georgian times the walls became a fashionable walkway around the city, completed with the construction of the Wishing Steps in 1785. The main city gates were removed to allow access for coaches and were replaced by grand archways. In the 1830s, a section of wall was knocked down when an access road was built to the new Grosvenor Bridge. Another section was removed and bridged over for the railway in 1845. When Castle Drive was built alongside the river a short section of wall was removed and the old Shipgate was moved to Grosvenor Park, then, with the increased use of the motor car, an inner ring road was driven through the north wall in the 1960s. Today, visitors can still walk around the unique and almost complete wall around the city.

WALK THE WALLS

The city can be circumnavigated by using the city walls. This guide splits it into four quarters. **Walk around the city walls from any main gateway to the next or follow the complete circuit 2km around the city.** On the way, you will see ancient and modern gates and towers. Watch the life of the busy shopping centre from the Eastgate Clock, leave the walls to visit the Roman amphitheatre or take a boat trip on the River Dee. Visit the Castle, watch the horse races on the Roodee or be a 'gongoozler' watching narrowboats climb the staircase lock on the Chester Canal. Imagine King Charles watching the defeat of his army or take a look at the falcons on the Deans Field (Cathedral green).

Instructions for sloped access are given at the beginning of each quarter.

Eastgate to Northgate (Cathedral and Civil War)
Sloped access beside the belltower (St Werburgh Street). Return and exit from here or by Kaleyards Gate (leading to Frodsham Street).

The ornamental clock on the Eastgate was built for Queen Victoria's Jubilee in 1897 but, like all public works, it took longer than expected and cost more money. Finally a local solicitor paid for the clock mechanism and it was erected in 1899, just in time for Victoria's 80th birthday. Until 1973, when electric winding was introduced, the firm of J B Joyce wound the clock each week. In 1992 the whole mechanism was replaced with an electric one. Before digital cameras, visitors used a tonne of paper each year just printing photos of this colourful highlight to the city.

The medieval gateway here, incorporating the Roman one, was too small for coaches and was demolished in 1768. In medieval times everyone entering with goods to sell had to pay a toll:

Of eney lode of salte entringe at the saide gate – a farthing
All soe of eny lode of coles entringe at the said gate – one
colebronde
Allsoe for eny lode of eathen potte – one potte
Allsoe for eny lode entringe with woode to be solde – one
bough nother a worse or a better
And for every horselode entringe with hay, one handeful

From the Eastgate, walk north (anticlockwise). Here the Wall is on its original Roman course and the footings are Roman.

You soon reach the Cathedral, its freestanding belltower and Garden of Remembrance. Until 1341 this was the Abbey of St Werburgh. The west face of the Cathedral shows the extensive restoration carried out by Sir George Gilbert Scott who was entrusted with major Gothic Revival works of the time. William Morris, founder of the Society for the Protection of Ancient Buildings, thought Scott destroyed many ancient buildings with little thought for their texture or substance.

The freestanding Addleshaw Tower, built in 1975, holds 13 of the cathedral bells.

The pattern in the garden represents a medal and ribbon in memory of the 22nd Cheshire Regiment soldiers who gave their lives in World War II.

To the right is Frodsham Street Car Park. Once used to grow hops for the abbey's brewery and cabbages for the monks, later the horse paddock for the Hop Pole Inn, it was saved from becoming the site of an electric power station and swimming baths in the late 19th century through its purchase by the Dean and Chapter as a public open space. They, however, had not foreseen the growth of the automobile industry and might today be shocked by its current use.

Stop by the next slope. An anchor cut into the outer wall 692 feet from the south wall of King Charles Tower in the distance, by a master mason of Chester and the owner of a nearby timberyard, celebrates the launch of the Great Eastern steam paddleship with a length of 692 feet launched in 1858 by Isambard Kingdom Brunel. The double-hulled ship was four times the size of other ships of the period and made completely from iron. One wonders if these two gentlemen, like thousands of others, went to the launch or just read about it in the paper.

692ft anchor mark GE

Below you is the Kaleyards Gate. Originally built for the monks to attend to their vegetable gardens in the 13th century, it was used as a sally port to attack the enemy (Parliamentarians) in the Civil War during the mid-17th century. Every night it is still closed after ancient custom at 9pm by the Cathedral, a quarter hour after the single curfew bell, still in the Cathedral Tower, is tolled.

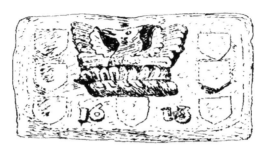

The phoenix on King Charles Tower GE

At the northeast corner of the wall stands the King Charles Tower. The phoenix carving is the emblem of the Painters, Glaziers, Embroiderers and Stationers Company, a city guild who held their meetings here and, in 1613, were given permission to repair the roof which was *uncouered with leade and rayne discending upon and into the same.*

However, during the Civil War, the guild met in safer Watergate Street while the tower was used for defence. In the Civil War turf ramparts were built to strengthen the city wall. Dead or injured bodies could quickly be removed with no rear wall on the parapet.

King Charles I watched from the top as his beaten Cavaliers pulled back from the Battle of Rowton Moor into the suburbs, then he took refuge in what he thought was the safer Cathedral Tower. He was proved wrong again when a musket ball killed the captain standing next to him. The king retreated to Wales leaving the city holding out until starvation took place the following year.

In 1854 a Mr Benjamin Huxley was allowed to rent the top floor at a rent of 2s6d a year provided that he *'only use it as an observatory'.*

Below, the Chester Canal was started in 1772. It is said that the contractors for the cut made a saving when, instead of having to cut the canal through solid rock, they only had to remove centuries of rubbish tipped over the walls since Roman times. Unfortunately the canal ended at Nantwich without joining the main network so that, only eight years later, shares in the canal company were worthless. It was only when the Ellesmere Canal Company joined it in 1795 that it began to flourish. The companies merged, and merged again into the Shropshire Union.

On his stroll around the walls in 1872, American writer, Henry James, saw *'burly watermen in smocks and breeches'.*

At the first building on your left is the entrance to Rufus Court and the steps down to Alexanders Beer Garden. This small shopping courtyard with its own jazz theatre won an award for its internal row design imitating the traditions of the medieval city. Take a quick look before continuing.

Opposite, carefully look over the wall ramparts to see the top course of the Roman wall below. This is the best section of the surviving Roman defence. From here can be seen the top of the carved cornice and rebated foundation stone to support the parapet wall. Below (view safely from the Northgate Bridge below) are thirteen courses without mortar on a chamfered plinth.

To leave the walls here, go down the steps through Rufus Court, or the steps by the Northgate and turn left to the city centre. The only sloped exits are by returning to the Cathedral.

Terracotta frontage of the Westminster Coach Works

Northgate to Watergate (Canal and Old Port)

Unfortunately there is no wheelchair access from the Northgate to St Martin's Gate (the bridge across St Martin's Way). The only sloped access to the later section of wall is opposite the former Infirmary 1763 on City Walls Road where the wall is alongside the pavement.

The earlier Northgate on this site contained the remains of the Roman gateway in it and the city gaol beside it. On 30th May 1578 the whole company of city butchers were imprisoned here for not suppling enough meat to citizens while forming a confederacy against country butchers. To be incarcerated in the airless, dark cells was not a pleasant fate and they were released on the 13th June after their humble submission to the mayor.

The Bridge of Sighs GE
Prisoners condemned to die suffered the 'drop' at the gaol after they had crossed the narrow bridge from their last visit to the chapel in the Bluecoat Hospital.

From the Northgate walk westwards (anticlockwise) above the Liverpool Arms. The Bluecoat Hospital is built on a site outside the walls, formerly occupied by the medieval Hospital of St John the Baptist. Pensioners later housed here were given *a good loaf daily, a great dish of pottage, a piece of flesh or fish and half a gallon of competant ale.* There are still almshouses at the rear of the building, added when the hospital was enlarged in 1854. The building of 1717 incorporated the Bluecoat School, the first charity school built outside London by the Society for the Promotion of Christian Knowledge.

Further along, in the park below, are the rebuilt capping stones on the Roman Wall shown on page 15.

You soon reach a square tower. Morgan's Mount is named after a captain in the Civil War who sited his cannon here. From this point, centuries earlier, the Roman wall would have turned southwards. You are about to follow the extension west built in the 10th century to fortify the Saxon burgh, which created the foremost medieval city in northwest England.

Below, on the canal, Northgate Locks were cut out of sandstone. Originally there were five leading down to the river but when the Wirral Arm of the Ellesmere Canal was cut from the corner below, a new course led down to the river through the lower basin.

Pass a half-round tower. Formerly the Goblin Tower, it was later named Pemberton's Parlour after a rope manufacturer (Pemberton) who watched his men working from the walls.

Telford's Warehouse, now a canalside pub, was named after Thomas Telford, General Agent, Surveyor, Architect and Overlooker of the Works on the canal. The original Ellesmere Canal Tavern was next door. Its proprietor did a brisk business running a fast packet boat from Liverpool from here in the 19th century. As well as food on the boat, the inn offered '...*good Beds, Wines, Spirituously malt liquors for the entertainment of families, Travellers & the public in general whose favors he humbly solicits assuring them it will be his constant study to merit their Approbation and support.*'

The Dee Basin entrance to the canal *(old engraving)*

Below you the canal turns north as you reach two corner towers. The closer one, pockmarked with the damage from musket balls during the Civil War, is the strangely named Bonewaldesthorne's Tower. In medieval times the River Dee travelled through the arch crossing the span from the walls to the Water Tower - a port watch tower built in 1322. The boat-shaped building beyond the tower is a scout hut.

The River Dee was canalised in the18th century. The wharves for the port and the Harbourmaster's House lie beyond the modern buildings on its altered course. A guide of 1851 noted the scenery from here: *The beautiful view of the winding Dee and the picturesque country on its banks is most delightful and cannot fail to excite very pleasurable emotions.*

Chester Quay (old engraving)

The Water Tower Gardens hold one ancient artefact, a bluestone that may be the 'Glover's Stone', moved here from a noted boundary between the city limits and the township of Gloverstone that had, at its hub, the old Chester Castle with the shire headquarters. Criminals or vagabonds were handed over *...att glovers stoune to such officer of the Cittie of Chester, in and from hence to whipp them through the Citie.*

Continue on the walls just above Castle Drive. The original castle mound is probably Norman; Henry II started rebuilding the original wooden structure with stone in 1245. Grosvenor Bridge with its single span stone arch was the longest in the world when it was opened by Princess Victoria in 1832 to the sound of a 21 gun salute. The bridge, to your right, the Propylaeum (castle entrance) designed in Greek Revivalist style and the modern castle to your left, were by Thomas Harrison. His other claim to fame is that he persuaded Lord Elgin to collect Greek antiquities. The Elgin Marbles were given to the British Museum and have caused controversy ever since.

Thomas Harrison's model bridge built to display the design before it was built, now situated below the wall on Castle Drive. GE

At the end of the wall turn left along the road to reach the Bridgegate and the old Dee Bridge. There was once another small gate on the river's edge known as the Shipgate. Its arch is now in the Grosvenor Park. On the far side of the Bridgegate was another gate, the Caple Gate or horsegate where horses could get to the river edge to drink.

Position of the Shipgate marked in the slope to the Bridgegate GE

Beside the bridge is the first hydro-electric station built in a city to power a city, with three turbines running in 1913 supplying a third of the city's requirements at that time, at a fifth of the cost of the coal-fired generators. It is on the site of the former Dee flour mills immortalised in the 'Miller of Dee' written by Bickerstaff in the 18th century, "I care for nobody, no not I, if nobody cares for me". The miller's song is based on the accusations that millers took more than their share of grain in payment.

The Old Dee Bridge GE

The Old Dee Bridge is near the site of the Roman bridge into the city. On the far side of the river, in the park, is a Roman statue of the goddess Minerva, who was probably set there to bless the safety of Romans crossing the river. This Roman idol survived destruction because people once thought it depicted the Virgin Mary but the owl on her shoulder should have given it away.

Turn left up Bridge Street to the city centre or continue along the next section of wall over the Bridgegate.

Detail on the Bridgegate GE

Bridgegate to Eastgate (River Dee and Amphitheatre)

Disabled access is severely limited on this section of the walls as each of the four ramps only serves a short section of wall. There is one at the Bridgegate, one from the junction of Park Street and Duke Street (steep), one by lift from Pepper Street Car Park, the other from the Grosvenor Precinct.

A more interesting route for wheelchairs or those who want to avoid steps can be found by continuing along the riverbank for 200 metres then turning left up through the Roman Gardens to the Newgate. Do not go through the gate but turn right to the amphitheatre and, using the pedestrian lights, first left up St John Street to the Eastgate.

The old Bridgegate had a large square tower built on its centre in 1600. This, combined with pipes from upstream and a water wheel on the weir, pumped water into the city, the first such system outside London. In the Civil War the tower was destroyed. When Daniel Defoe visited the city in 1690, water had to be carried up the hill in leather vessels on horseback. However, in 1692, a new octagonal water tower was built on the west side of the gate.

In 1731 the clerk of the works suffered a dreadful accident when he *stood upon a plank in the water engine to oyl the brasses there he accidentally slipped and fell down headlong under the crank ...he received a mortall wound or was crushed and bruised by the said crank that he instantly dyed.* Later, the waterworks were replaced upstream but the tower remained until the present arched gateway was built.

Tyrer's Tower 1600-45

Follow the wall eastwards (anticlockwise) past the remains of the round tower. Ignore the next steps on your right unless you want to go down to the riverside (the Groves). The steps are named after the city's top judge: the Recorder.

Go up the 'Wishing Steps'. If you can run up and down them whilst holding your breath your wish may come true. The original legend was only for young women looking for husbands but the tale has grown with the telling.

To your right are the Roman Gardens which can be accessed by going down the slope on your left then through the small gate under the wall. Displays of Roman columns stones and *pilae* from the Roman baths create a long park between the river and the Newgate.

To the left is the Albion pub, full of World War I memorabilia. Further on are the six remaining 'nine houses', with their unusual solid base and timber-framed uppers.

Above the car park is a lion statue from the former brewery on the site.

Unless you want to descend the steps to visit the amphitheatre, cross the modern Newgate. This gate was built to widen access in 1938. Next to it stands the former Newgate also known as the 'Peppergate' or 'Wolfgate', rebuilt in 1608. Its unusual name may come from the Norse personal name *Ulfaldi*, or from the carved wolf's head above the former gate, the wolf was a symbol on the coat of arms of Chester's first Norman earl, Hugh d'Avranches (Hugh Lupus).

The gate now leads to the ruin of the Southeast Angle Tower, originally inside the Roman fort: a collapse of the Roman wall led to the new line of the wall further back.

From here the course of the southern Roman wall followed the present Pepper Street. The section of wall you have just walked was an Anglo-Saxon addition to enlarge the fortified city. By lengthening the city walls on the north and east to reach the river, the Saxons quadrupled the cities protected area.

The Wolfgate, also known as the Peppergate or Newgate rebuilt in 1609

Just beyond a tower is the entrance to the Grosvenor Precinct. Partially destroyed in the Civil War, Thimbleby's Tower now has a mock-medieval roof.

Steps on your left head down to Eastgate Street and Foregate Street. If you want to continue around the walls go to page 4.

Eastgate Street *Old engraving*

CHRONICLE OF CHESTER WALLS

AD/CE c50s/60s A small primary Roman fort may have existed at Chester.

c74 Roman fortress walls made from timber with turf ramparts and ditch by II Legion.

c102 Roman stone walls started by XX Legion.

c200 Wall building renewed as XX Legion returns from Hadrian's Wall. Roman gravestones used in north wall during third century.

Gravestone found in the north Wall *GE*

'To the spirits of the departed, Manius Aurelius Nepos, centurion of the Twentieth Legion, Valeria Victrix, lived 50 years; his most dutiful wife had this set up.'

c383 Magnus Maximus takes much of the legions abroad in a revolt against Rome. They never return but a garrison appears to have held Chester up to the 390's.

c417 Roman General and Bishop, St Germanus, deposes Vortigern (great King) the last Ruler of all Britain, accusing him and the British bishops of heresy. Chester or adjacent North Wales may have been the location for this, and at least one Bishop was based nearby. Thereafter the country deteriorates into petty tribalism, and Saxons begin to overrun (what is now) England.

c418 Anglo-Saxon Chronicle records that "*This year the Romans collected all the treasures that were in Britain, and some they hid in the earth…*"

c475 In legend, Arthur fights his ninth battle at 'the city of the legions' (may have been Chester or Caerleon).

c603 Synod of the British church held in Chester suggests that the city has become an ecclesiastical centre.

C613/6 Battle of Chester: King Ethelfrith of Northumbria defeats the Welsh (British) and slays 2000 monks from Bangor-on-Dee.

c660 St Peter and St Paul's Church founded inside the walls on the site of the present Cathedral.

c689 Giraldus states that St John the Baptist Church is founded (outside the walls).

894 Alfred besieges Danes in Chester.

C907/12 Aethelflaeda creates a fortified burgh by the simple method of extending the north and east walls to the River Dee thus creating a fortified burgh (it is now believed that some of this extension may have been based on a similar Roman extension).

c1057 During an attack on the city by King Gruffydd (Gruffydd-ap-Llewellyn) the remains of St Werburgh were carried onto the walls and are said to have *'struck the king blind'*. A stained glass window in the Cathedral commemorates this tale.

1086 The Domesday Book records that: for the repair of the city walls and bridge the reeve used to call up one man from each hide in the county. The lord of any man who failed to come was fined 40s shared between the king and earl.

c1120 Bridgegate and Shipgate built.

c1150 Western walls built, partly along Roman 'quay' wall.

1275 Monks build 'Kaleyards Gate' to reach their vegetable gardens.

1303 Wolfgate/Peppergate mentioned as 'Wofuldegate'.

1307 Murage duty taken to keep the walls in good repair.

1321 Tolls at the Watergate include: *'of every horselode of mussels one little dishful... of every horselode of great fishe, a quarter of a fishe or the headd or one penny'*.

1322   Port Watch Tower (now called the Water Tower) built to extend the walls to the new course of the River Dee for £100.

1499 Midsummer Watch Parade started, a colourful parade that linked the walls, the church, the civil authority and the people. There was also a Christmas Eve Watch: a candlelit procession would go from the Mayor's house to the Common Hall where the keys to the city gates would be given to the mayor who, in turn, entrusted them to the watchmen who would keep the city safe over Yuletide.

1569 The two city sheriffs were fined £10 towards repairing the walls.

1573 The Newgate /Peppergate/Wolfgate is locked after Mayor Aldersey's daughter elopes through it; later in the year it was just locked at night. This gave rise to a Chester saying "locking the

Peppergate after the daughter had gone", similar to the saying about locking the stable door after the horse has bolted.
1589 Harre Tower on the medieval and Roman Eastgate rented to one of the city companies for an annual rent of 6d.
1599-1600 John Tyrer builds square tower in the centre of the Bridgegate as a water storage tower, pumping water up by a waterwheel on the Dee, and thence by pipe to the city.
1608/9 Wolfgate rebuilt.
1613 The companies of Barber Surgeons, Tallowchandlers and Wanchandlers together with the company of Painters, Glaziers Embroiderers and Stationers as tenants of the Phoenix Tower (now King Charles Tower) complained that it was *'uncoered with leade and rayne discending upon and into the same'* and petitioned the Assembly to let them repair it.
1620 more repairs on the Phoenix Tower.
1692/3 Phoenix (emblem of the Stationer's Company) carving by Randle Holme III put up on Phoenix Tower by Edward Nixon.
1640 Sep 18 City watch continued at night.
1642 Jan 1 (New Year started in March) Murengers request money to repair walls. Sep 6 100 marks assessed on citizens to repair walls.
1643 Nov 11 6 gates have 8 guards - 4 with muskets, 4 with halberds. Dec 1 Parliamentarian troops encircle city. Prince Maurice later relieves city.
1644 Chester siege resumed. King Charles later relieves city.
1645 The King, on the Phoenix Tower, watches his troops fight in the suburbs after losing the Battle of Rowton Moor. For safety he moves to the Cathedral Tower but even here his captain next to him is shot in the head.
Dec 30 After the King has fled, Brereton reports the complete encirclement of Chester.
Feb 3 The city surrendered (after having refused 9 times). Tyrer's water tower destroyed, Thimbleby's Tower (named after Lord, and Lady Thimbleby who died in Chester 1615) partially destroyed, breaches in the east wall.
1662 John Crewe released the right of tolls from the Eastgate to the Assembly in return for rent from the Roodeye.
1692 Hadley and Hopkins build octagonal water tower on west side of the Bridgegate to resupply the city with water.
1693 date with the initials RH (Randle Holme) carved into Kaleyards gate may have been the date of a rebuild.
1700 Recorder's steps built to the south wall.

1707 City Assembly made a grant of £1,000 to repair and re-flag the walls to make a walkway with an unfortified parapet. Morgan's Mount rebuilt.

1717 Bluecoat Hospital built outside Northgate.

1719 The unfortunately named Ann Edge falls from walls by Phoenix Tower.

1768 Eastgate pulled down, parts of Roman gate found. Aug 8th cornerstones of Eastgate arch laid by Aldermen, Mayor and sheriffs.

Thomas Boswell petitions to build steps to Abbey Green.

1769 Eastgate arch completed by Mr Hayden, funded by Richard Lord Grosvenor.

1772 Chester Canal started to be cut below walls. Workers find that the Roman ditch is full of rubbish.

1778 April 5th A huntsman of the Chester Harriers, for a wager, rides around the walls, leaping two turnstiles, in 9½ minutes.

1782 Bridgegate rebuilt as an arch by Joseph Turner.

1785 Wishing steps built.

1789 Turner builds new Watergate Arch.

1793 Turner builds 'Bridge of Sighs' to join Northgate Gaol to Bluecoat chapel for prisoners.

1808 Northgate Gaol demolished.Thomas Harrison builds Northgate arch commissioned by Robert, Second Earl Grosvenor.

1830 Morgan's Mount repaired.

1832 Grosvenor Road cuts through city walls to Grosvenor Bridge, the first new entrance to the city since medieval times.

1836 Tolls at city gates discontinued.

1838 Shipgate removed (now in Grosvenor Park)

1845-6 Chester and Holyhead Railway cut through northwestern corner of city walls and is bridged over.

1854 Copper rod and anchor carving with initials DS (District Surveyor) set in Bridgegate as a benchmark. Top floor of King Charles' Tower let as an observatory to Mr Benjamin Huxley for 2s6d per annum. Camera obscura mounted in Bonewaldesthorne's Tower by the Mechanics Institute.

1858 An anchor with '692Ft' carved 692 feet south of the southern wall of King Charles' Tower by Mr William Haswell, mason, and Mr Musgrave, timber-yard owner, to celebrate the launch of the Great Eastern, an enormous iron ship built by Brunel originally called The Leviathan.

1879 Tramway opened through Eastgate going from Chester

Station to Saltney, these were converted to electric trams just over 20 years later.

1879 Watch Tower by Wishing Steps taken down.

1881 I Matthews Jones, the city surveyor, finds Roman gravestones in North Wall near Phoenix Tower. They are stored in the Water Tower Gardens where some disappeared and others eroded. They are then recognised as the best preserved set of gravestones in Northern Europe and are now displayed at the Grosvenor Museum in a special gallery.

1894 Goblin Tower (later known as Pemberton's Parlour) rebuilt.

1899 Eastgate Clock started at 12.45 on Queen Victoria's 80th birthday, two years after it was designed for her Jubilee.

1903 Buffalo Bill photographed with 'cowboys and Indians' by the walls in the Roodeye for his 'Wild West' show.

1938 New Newgate built in mock medieval style to allow widened Pepper Street traffic but the wrong way round as the arrow slits face inwards.

1966 St Martin's Gate, an arch over the inner ring-road, opened by transport minister Barbara Castle.

1975 Addlestone Tower built beside Walls to house most of Cathedral bells, except the curfew bell, still in the Cathedral.

1984 New camera obscura fitted in Bonewaldesthorne's Tower.

1995 Rufus Court built adjoining walls with internal 'rows'.

2012 After an extensive survey both minor and major repairs to the walls begin.

2013 A new viewing platform built when King Charles Tower restored.

2014 'Friends of the walls' established.

The District Surveyor's benchmark of 1854 under the arch of the Bridgegate includes a set-in copper rod and a carved anchor. This was a forerunner to the later Ordnance Survey benchmarks used in mapping the whole of Britain GE

Corner of St Werburgh Street JH

SHOPPING ON CHESTER'S MEDIEVAL ROWS

To save space and increase shopping area, modern shopping malls are often built under cover on two floors. This 20th century idea was developed in Chester 700 years earlier.

However, not all the rows were two storeys, some were at ground level: Lorimers' Row (harness makers) under the Blue Bell dates back eight centuries; the modern St Werburgh's Row was built in 1935. Other cities had rows where certain tradesmen gathered – in 1634 it was ordered that all Goldsmiths in London were to be accommodated in Goldsmiths' Row in Cheapside. It is the two storey Rows that are unique to Chester.

When Edward I's armies started their Welsh campaign in 1277 Edward built a castle here then started an enormous castle-building scheme in Wales. Woodsmen, masons, carpenters and soldiers used the city as a base. The trade and building boom that resulted saw the two-tiered shops (Rows) that remain today. The king's master craftsman Richard Lenginour (the engineer) was probably instrumental in building work, as he settled here and became mayor of the city in 1305.

By 1278 *buttershops* stood on two levels at the corner of Eastgate Street and Northgate Street. A *corvyserrowe* (shoemakers' row) was on the second storey of Bridge Street West in 1346. Butchers shops *le flessherowe* existed on the second storey of Watergate Street North by 1345 with cellars below. Once, most of the street level shops were also vaults or cellars holding fine wines, cheeses and other wares. In fact the vault at 12 Bridge Street was only rediscovered under rubble in 1839.

Watergate Street South Row was *Welsh Row then Linen Row*, the setting for the Linen Market, while below was the Fish Board selling fresh fish to merchants and the public. *Ironmongers Row* was recorded in 1330 and 1550 in Northgate Street West but the main row here was *Shoemakers Row* replaced by Harrison's Commercial Newsrooms and a half-timbered Row set just above the street.

Catastrophically, in 1772, a hundredweight (50kg) of gunpowder was stored in a Watergate Street vault, when the city's fire

regulations forbade anything over two pounds (1kg) –
unfortunately a puppet show was taking place to an assembled
audience when the lot blew up killing the showman and 22
others, and this was on the 5th November.

Eastgate Street North Row became known as *Dark Row* because
the outside stalls, yet another set of shops, hid the light from the
footway. Another name for it was *Broken Shin Row* – owners had
no duty to make the surface flat and there were often steps
between individual owners' buildings.

**The Old Boot Inn on Dark Row (Eastgate Street Row North) was built
from secondhand timbers in the Civil War. Inside is a musket ball found
lodged in the beams.** *JH*

Even in the 17th century the Rows were an exciting place to shop.
If you could make your way along the creaky boards from one
shop to another you would have to dodge displays of goods on
the floor, walls and hanging from the rafters.

In the evenings, gangs of ruffians might gather in these dark lofts and wait, perhaps for a chance to cut a purse free from its owner. By 1673 *'all benches and showboards in the rows'* had to be *'made with hinges'* so that they could be folded up at night.

'Dark Row' Eastgate Street Row North *JH*

In 1656 Daniel King stated *'it is a goodly sight to see the numbers of fair shops that are in these Rows of Mercers, Grocers, Drapers and Haberdashers aspecially in the street called The Mercers Row'.* This is now Bridge Street Row East and yes, if you are shopping, you can still find clothes' shops here.

Daniel Defoe, in the early 18th century, thought the Rows *'old and ugly'* but his views of many towns on his tour of Britain were often tinged with disappointment. Wesley, on his visits to preach in St John Street during 1752, found the covered Rows were *'the greatest convenience'.* For a man used to preaching outside in all weathers that is a compliment indeed.

One of the oldest shopfronts on the Rows is at Bridge Street. In 1803 George Lowe, goldsmith had two shops at *Pentice Row* (now demolished) but moved to Bridge Street Row East where the shop can still be found selling quality silver. Look out also for the Georgian Tea Rooms, formerly a cheese shop on Northgate Street Row East.

Black and white timbering above Bridge Street West Row   *JH*

The Victorian era saw many of the shopfronts rebuilt in black and white style. Some were completely new and some copied from the original designs. By 1894 some of the traders were fed up with the council's delay in providing electric lighting. Jos Beckett, from a shop in Eastgate Street complained that *'the gas is very injurious to fine fabrics... besides being often of poor quality'*. However, electricity came to the city in 1896 with the construction of the Chester Electric Lighting Station in Crane Street.

Fifteen years later, now able to light indoor shops efficiently with a unit of electricity at 6d (2.5p) Chester architect W T Lockwood built St Michael's Row off Bridge Street Row East for the Duke of Westminster. This Edwardian arcade now connects with the Grosvenor Shopping Centre which lies between Eastgate Street and Pepper Street.

Although many of the frontages are new, some of the vaults date back to Norman times, and inside the buildings were great halls built from the 13th century onwards. Each building has its own story to tell. Visit some of the shops in the vaults; The Falcon; and Olde Leche House, the ninth bay in Watergate Street South Row (Sofa Workshop) to see information inside. *(Also see History.)*

From the Cross there are four streets with first-storey Rows that can be accessed for shopping. You will find an enormous range of individual retailers, cafes and pubs as you follow in the footsteps of shoppers over 700 years.

Wheelchair access to the rows on Eastgate Street South and Bridge Street East can be made via the Grosvenor Shopping Centre, exiting through St Michaels' Row.

Access to Watergate Street North is via a slope at Crook Street; Watergate Street South Row and Bridge Street West Row by Old Hall Passage off Old Hall Place, and a slope off Pierpoint Lane.

Eastgate Street North Row can be accessed from Godstall Lane off St Werburgh Street.

The Grosvenor Precinct has a slope on Eastgate Street and a lift at Pepper Street and another from the car park in Newgate Street.

Church of St John the Baptist. *King Ethelred may have founded a wooden church here in c689AD, possibly on an earlier Christian site. The first stone building and foundation coins underneath it were placed here in c912AD by Ethelfleda. Under the Anglo-Saxons it became an important 'minster', then under the Normans, Chester's first Cathedral. When the bishopric moved to Coventry building works slowed down. After Henry VIII created the current cathedral, his daughter Elizabeth I did a deal granting the building to the parishioners in exchange for the lead off its roof for her soldiers.*

During the Civil War snipers used the west tower to shoot into the city. In 1861 this tower collapsed with 'a long drawn out rattle' accompanied by 'the cacophonic clash of bells' luckily before the Good Friday service was to take place. **St John's Trail, inside the gates, explores the ruins. Look also for the wooden coffin set up beside an arch for effect in the early 19th century.**

ditch and dyke *The Saxon version of Hadrian's Wall or perhaps the Antonine Wall, as it was made of earth and turf, Offa's Dyke runs from Chepstow to Treuddyn, near Mold; Wat's Dyke, probably a later extension, from Oswestry via Wrexham to Holywell.* **The nearest good section of Offa's Dyke can be seen at Bersham, near Wrexham SJ297495 on the Clywedog Trail.**

extend the walls *Extensions to the Roman walls in medieval times are explained on page 16.*

St Werburgh's remains *or relics were said to have miraculous powers. The legend of St Werburgh tells how, in her life, she restored a cooked goose and set it free after admonishing the flock for eating corn. Her remains are said to have repelled the Welsh king from Chester and stopped a city fire. The Norman shrine to her was smashed in the Reformation but restored in 1876.* **See Cathedral feature.**

St Peter's Church *at* **The Cross** *stands on part of the site of the Roman Principia. As well as having Chester's first public clock it also had, from as early as 1288, a wooden town hall leaning on it known as the Pentice, rebuilt in stone, then demolished for road widening at the beginning of the 19th century.*

Go to page 55

The importance of Chester as a border city and St John's Church,also known as the 'church of the holy rood' after the legend of the holy cross washed up here, was confirmed when King Edgar, crowned in Bath, was **rowed up the River Dee** by eight minor kings, to a service of allegiance in the church.

The Anglo-Saxons traded with the Norse, the Irish and Europe. Mints in the city produced more **silver coin** than anywhere else in England during the first half of the 10th century.

Norse influence here can be found in names on the coin, a church dedicated to **St Olave** (the martyred Norwegian king who died in 1030), and in the names John Gunde and Agnes Outhcarle on the sale of a stone house to Peter the Clerk (later in the 13th century).

After the Norman invasion, William's **Domesday Book** recorded 487 substantial houses in the city before the conquest along with local laws and import duties.

Ruled by Norman Sword

After holding out against William, the city was severely ravaged with 205 houses destroyed. A succession of seven Norman earls ruled over Cheshire but, with a wealth of other land, nearly a third of England in size, did not always live in Chester.

The first ruthless earl Hugo (Hugh Lupus) who was said to have a *'retinue more like an army than a household'* and was later named *Hugh the fat* by the Welsh, nevertheless established **St Werburgh's Benedictine Abbey**, and, perhaps worried about an unholy life, is said to have become a monk in his last days.

His son Richard, along with Henry I's son, died when their ship sank. Earl Ranulph converted the Wirral farmlands into his own hunting forest. His son, Ranulph II, ended up capturing King Stephen, and his huge landholdings were virtually run as a seperate state. Hugh II fought against King Henry but was pardoned. Ranulph III built **Beeston Castle** after returning from the Crusades. The last earl, John (the Scot), only received a small portion of his father's lands but died five years later. Chester reverted to King Henry II's ownership in 1237.

Go to page 56

silver coin   *There were seven small mints in the city before the Norman Conquest. There were Norse, Welsh, Irish and German moneyers in the cosmopolitan city. **The Castle Esplanade coin hoard of over 700 coins and other silver, buried in c970 and found in 1950 can only be seen by scholars at the Grosvenor Museum by strict prior arrangement.***

St Olave   *The stone former church is on Lower Bridge Street.*

Domesday Book   *Ownership of land and property together with Chester's laws from Saxon times were recorded by the Normans in 1086. Burglars could be fined £4 on holy days, £2 at other times; a similar fine applied to killing a man. Unlawful intercourse by a widow cost her 20 shillings, by a girl 10 shillings, but women were protected from violence in their houses by a £2 fine. Murderers of freemen were outlawed and their goods taken. Tax dodgers were fined 10 shillings.*

St Werburgh's Abbey *is now the Cathedral. **See Cathedral feature.** As well as the abbey, Chester had three friaries and a nunnery. Dominicans (black friars) had come to the city by 1236 and were given leave, by Richard II, to grind their corn toll-free at the Dee Mills. In 1238 Franciscans (grey friars) came here and soon built a house and chapel using stone from the castle ditch given to them by Henry II who ended up with a better defence into the bargain. Local fishermen then kept their buildings in good repair in exchange for storage of nets and tackle. Carmelites (white friars), here from 1237, wore undyed cassocks and took vows of poverty, chastity and obedience.*

Carving of St Benedict under the Abbey Gate

Beeston Castle *can be reached by Beeston Station via Crewe.*

*The castle was used as an insignia for the Chester Canal Company's official seal, (kept at the Grosvenor Museum) now on the **commemorative stone at Northgate Lock.***

Go to page 57

MEDIEVAL CITY LIFE

Through the Middle Ages **Chester Port** flourished, importing wines from Gascon, Spanish iron, sheepskin, furs, fruits; exporting salt and cheese, as well as raisins, nuts and spices to Ireland. Custom duty was paid on wine, iron and hides however city traders were exempt from customs, but not port tolls on their own goods. Despite the River Dee becoming silted up and ships having to dock on the Wirral coast (part of Chester Port) the number of ships doubled from the 15th to 16th centuries.

The city merchants formed **guilds** and elected a mayor and sheriffs, performed the spectacular **Mystery Plays** and **Midsummer Watch** in conjunction with the Abbey, and built the medieval city and its unique **Rows**.

The Rows of two-tiered shops and vaults ran along the front of several great halls such as those at **Three Old Arches, The Falcon** and **Booth Mansion, Leche House** and **38-42 Watergate Street.**

The city was a busy place to shop. With no means of keeping fresh food, each household needed to buy fresh meat, fish and bread on a regular basis. For larger houses it would be the servants who went to shop, catching local gossip and listening to the **crier or bellman's** proclamations at the High Cross.

Like the colourfully painted and guilded Cross, the townspeople wore bright colours, with linen or woollen clothes and fur trims. With Chester as a main fur trading port the latter was easy to come by. All goods had to be brought from the country or the port by wagon or packhorse. Long teams of these would venture out into the foothills of Wales, while drovers bringing their cattle and other animals to market drove them up beside the Dee then along Cow Lane (Frodsham Street) up until the mid-20th century.

Country people from areas like Wrexham, Farndon, Tattenhall and Christleton would walk or ride into the city, starting at dawn to get here early enough to catch the markets opening.

Fairs and markets were held in the city streets, traders from outside the city paying tolls and fees (see pages 26,35 & 57).

Go to page 58

Chester Port   *It is recorded that, before the Conquest, if the King's reeve ordered those who had marten pelts, they had not to sell to anyone until they had first been shown to him and he had bought, whoever neglected this paid a fine of 40 shilling. Ships sailed up the Dee as far as the Old Dee Bridge where they could unload or load skins. There were also quays just outside the Watergate. Tolls at the gate in 1321 included 'of every horselode of mussells one little dishfull... of every horselode of great fishe, a quarter of a fishe or the headd or one penny'. The earl of Chester had a right to a 'prise' of all wine imports at the port which included the Wirral quays. (Chester was one of only five English wine ports.) He would take one 'tun' from the front and one from the rear of the boat – 2268 litres in all.*

guilds   *Powerful merchants in the city had almost exclusive rights for retail sales. The guildsmen had to be freemen of the city, and take an oath to serve Chester and the king. To become a freeman one had to be born the son of a freeman, purchase membership or be given honorary membership.*

__Shoemakers' Row before demolition__ (see page 15) G Pickering 1830

Go to page 59

At the annual **fairs** even vagabonds and outlaws could ask for the city's protection, signified by a hanging carved wooden hand or glove on St Peter's Church, unless they carried out further misdemeanours. Strict rules and pricing for some foodstuffs were set for **markets** by the City Assembly. Seafish was sold at an open Fishboard in Watergate Street where citizens could buy before 9am, fishmongers after but 'foreign fishers' (ie anyone outside Chester) could only retail after 10am. It was illegal to 'regrate' (buy up stocks and sell at inflated prices) or 'forestall' (buy or sell before reaching market).

'Foreigners' also had to pay special tolls, for example at the new **Common Hall** *'every Kendall man... with eny clothe... pay for every pak 1d'.*

Henry VII's Great Charter of 1506 confirmed the power of the city council, excepting the **Castle** and **Gloverstone**, Education was given by the monks of the abbey or private tutors such as Henry Dowes, tutor of Gregory, Thomas Cromwell's son in Chester, who reported to Thomas, *"I tell him... history of the Romans...",* but Gregory was more interested in other matters, *"...to hawk, to hunt and shoot in his longbow... he seemeth to be thereunto given by nature".*

Henry VIII closed down the abbey and its schooling, replacing it with today's Cathedral and the King's School. If you consider that the former Abbot became the new Dean while ten monks were kept on for new duties, while many estates were sold at knockdown prices to local gentry, it is unlikely that, apart from those with strong religious views, many citizens suffered.

However, Chester did see two martyrs to their religions: In 1555, under the Roman Catholic Queen Mary, George Marsh, a widower with children was accused of heresy and preaching Luther's doctrine. He was condemned to death and led to Gallows Hill in Boughton reading his bible, where he was burned at the stake. Much later, in 1679, it was John Plessington, a practising Roman Catholic priest who was found guilty of High Treason and hanged, drawn and quartered at Gallows Hill.

Under both Henry VIII and Elizabeth I, those who still remained Roman Catholic had to worship and hide in secret compartments, such as the priest holes at Leche House and Boughton Hall, when searches were made. As late as 1737 a priest, Edward

Go to page 60

Mystery plays   *In conjunction with the abbey, the city guilds performed 24 pageants telling bible stories. Each guild performed one play, which was acted on wheeled stages taken to the streets of the city. By 1475 this was a three day event. Early plays included an exhortation to each company to perform their act well. The plays were eventually banned as 'popery' under Elizabeth I, although they were revived in the 20th century and are now usually performed every 5 years.*

Midsummer Watch   *During the mayorality of Erichard Goodman in 1499 the 'Wach on Midsummer Eve was first sett out'. This was a parade by the city guilds which took place in the years between the Mystery Plays. Like the Mystery Plays, the colourful noisy parades linked the church and civil authorities. In 1564 there were 4 gyants, 1 unikorne, 1 dramodarye, 1 luce, 1 camell, 6 hobby horses and 16 naked boys following the drum and city standard. In 1600 the Protestant mayor banned the parade but it was soon revived without the devil in feathers and the naked boys. The watch ended in 1678 and was revived in 1995.*

The Christmas Eve Watch *was a quieter affair with a candlelit procession to the Common Hall where the city gate keys were entrusted to the watchmen to keep the city safe over Yuletide.*

Rows *see **Shopping on Chester's Medieval Rows** page 40.*

vaults   *Eleventh to 14th century vaults can be seen in many of the shops below street level. Good examples at **11 Watergate Street, 28 Eastgate Street** and **12 Bridge Street.***

Three Old Arches   *Said to be the oldest stone shopfront in Britain, these arches in **Bridge Street** West Row may even date to the early 14th century. Behind them is a medieval hall, the largest structure ever found in the Rows.*

The Falcon & Leche House   *See **Alehouses** and **Shopping on Chester's Medieval Rows**. Leche House was rebuilt in the late 15th century and has a gallery within the shop on the Row. The house was used for 'illegal' Roman Catholic services during the 17th century and has a peep hole to watch out for the law.*

Booth Mansion   *Two medieval townhouses at **28-34 Watergate Street** were later altered and extended over the street in 1700. Its assembly rooms became fashionable for balls in the Georgian period.*

     Go to page 61

__Rows by the Cross__ JH

Hughes, was arrested for giving mass just across the Welsh border.

The new mayor, Henry Gee, ruled that all children over six years *'learne ther beliefe & other devocions prayers and learnings or els to such other good and vertuus laborure craft or occupacyon'.*

Many buildings from the 16th and 17th centuries have been restored including **Stanley Palace** *in lower Watergate Street and* **The Old Rectory** *in Bridge Street East.*

CIVIL WAR

When Charles I had dinner with the mayor in **Gamul House** during 1645 it was on his second and final visit. The city had supported him with two grants of 100lb of gold, melted down the city plate for silver coin and housed his troops on the way to Ireland. As a result the city lay under siege from the Cheshire MP

Go to page 62

crier & bellman *At one time the city had a crier, a day bellman, and a night bellman. Over the centuries the jobs combined until in the 20th century there was a bellman and crier once more. However history has repeated itself and when the last crier left, the bellman once again took both jobs. Today's crier can be found* **by the Cross** *in summer.*

Not only did the bellman lead funerals but also made public cries regarding retail sales, the races, and the Mystery Plays. In fact he or the crier were the announcer of news and legal notices.

fairs and **markets** **Today's markets are held by the Town Hall.** *The council still control and licence all markets and fairs in the city even computer fairs. The original Midsummer and Michaelmas fairs brought retailers from all over England. After the fairs the 'leavelookers' would ensure that non-guildsmen left the city.*

A cattle market used to be held along 'Cow Lane' the old name for Frodsham Street. Occasionally cattle would wander into shops by mistake. After 1704 the horse fair in the street was held in Foregate Street. Traders discussed their prices at the Boot Inn on the Horsetraders' bench in the rear bar. The sheriffs had to keep records of all horse sales along with a description of any horse, mare, gelding or colt sold, along with its vendor, purchaser and price. The earliest example comes from 1655: 'William Roberts of Handbridge... hath sould unto Matthew Scott of Dublin gentleman one sorril bay nagge wuth three white feet and a white face which ambles'.

Cows in Watergate Street 19th century

Go to page 63

The Falcon *J S Prout 1840*

Brereton, with his Parliamentary forces. The present Falcon Inn was the home of Sir Richard Grosvenor and had its Row enclosed to make his family's life in the war-torn city more comfortable, while the Boot Inn is said to have been built from timbers from houses knocked down outside the city as part of Chester's defences.

Charles lost his last Cheshire Battle (see Walls page 17) and left the city. Brereton wrote, *'the beseiged in Chester remain obstinate'* while inside the walls his mortar attacks were *'great grenadoes like so many demi-phaetons threaten to set the city if not the world alight'*. By 1646, having refused to surrender nine times, with Lord Byron at the head of the city's defences, having only spring water and boiled wheat for lunch – the citizens had already eaten their dogs – a treaty was signed. The mills and the waterworks lay in ruins and not one house *'from the Eastgate to the middle of Watergate Street'* had escaped the heavy bombing.

Go to page 64

Common Hall   *Needless to say the medieval Common Hall was in the street named after it, but in 1545 the citizens purchased the old Chapel of St Nicholas (**St Werburgh Street** Superdrug) with the profits made from an import of Spanish iron. All wholesale goods had to be sold here.*

Castle & Gloverstone   *The township around the Castle was known as Gloverstone. The city's bylaws did not apply there so that it was an ideal place for black market sales. Several glovers lived in the area. (See **Walk the Walls and Bluestone** (page 46)).*

Stanley Palace   *Lovingly restored by Chester Civic Trust, this 1591 timber-framed hall with its long gallery (**below the traffic lights in Watergate Street**) is open to the public when not hired.*

The Old Rectory   *The brown facade of this 17th century house in **Bridge Street** was matched to the original carving.*

Gamul House   *is now the Brewery Tap in **Lower Bridge Street**. If you want to recreate history you could always try inviting the Lord Mayor.*

Boot Inn   *See **Alehouses**.*

Lower Bridge Street   *W Tasker c1839*

Go to page 65

The exultant Puritan Parliamentary forces let loose in the city, despite the treaty, destroyed religious icons including the **High Cross**. In 1649 King Charles was proclaimed a traitor at its base.

As if that were not enough to bear, the starved citizens bore the full brunt of the plague, with 2099 people dead from the summer of 1647 to the following spring. Hardly surprising then that one family who survived put up the motto 'God's Providence is mine inheritance' on **God's Providence House** in 1652 (now rebuilt).

In 1656, three 'witches' were dutifully tried by the Puritans, found guilty and hanged, their remains buried in the Castle ditch.

Chester Port declined. With most ships from the colonies now going to Liverpool, larger ships were needed on the transatlantic slave run and they could not get up the Dee. However, Cheshire merchants were still involved in the demeaning trade until its abolition in 1807, and even then made money from the slave colonies.

However, it was not all doom and gloom. In 1652, four 'waits' employed by the city were given livery every three years. They were paid 10 shillings to play in the city streets at Christmas. In 1650 **Nine Houses** were built. When **Owen Jones**, a local butcher, died he left charitable bequests that continue to this day.

RESTORATION

The destruction of the city and the restoration of the Monarchy led to a new wave of restoration in Chester. The Bridgegate Tavern, now the **Bear & Billet**, the Old House in Whitefriars, Bridge House (**Oddfellows Hall**) and the **Dutch Houses** were built and freshwater reinstated by building a new octagonal water tower on the west side of the Bridgegate. Two dilapidated houses in Watergate Street restored by Lady Kilmorey became the single **Bishop Lloyd's** House. At the end of the 17th century a new **Exchange** (town hall) was built.

GEORGIAN SOCIETY

In the 18th century the city grew in stature and population if not in size. Fire regulations were enforced to ensure that *flaxdressers... do not smoke Tobacco... in their flaxshops* and that *gorse, furze*

Go to page 66

The Exchange 1698-1862 *G Pickering 1829*

High Cross *In 1606, 'A Stranger did Dance and Vault upon a rope, which was fastened a great height above the ground, overthwart the high Crosse which did seem strange to the beholders'.*

First recorded in 1377 today's Cross incorporates just two parts of the original. Destroyed in the Civil War, parts remained hidden until 1806. A reconstructed version was erected in the Roman Gardens then moved to its present position in 1975. However, the dull stone that you can see is just a shadow of its gilded and painted former self which had figures of saints and probably the Virgin Mary.

God's Providence House *is in **Watergate Street South**.*

Nine Houses *Six of the half-timbered houses remain in Park Street.*

*A plaque to **Owen Jones** is on the bank by the Eastgate.*

65

Go to page 67

or faggots for baker's ovens stayed outside the city. (Now it's storage for buses at the new bus station.)

In 1719 a silver oar was made for the Mayor as a symbol of his Admiral status on the Dee, and in 1733 work to straighten, widen and deepen the river was started. Only about 100 ships a year sailed up the completed navigation yet visitors still used the city as a destination and as a stopping place on their journeys. Handel practised his Messiah here on his way to Ireland. At the end of the 18th century crowds gathered to see Lunardi fly his balloon from the Castle yard; followed a few days later by a Lieutenant French; then the local owner of Hoole Hall, who made it as far as Warrington. In 1824 another famous balloonist, Mr Sadler, took off from the Castle yard and flew 9 miles to Utkinton.

A four horse coach first ran from the **Pied Bull** to Birkenhead for the Liverpool ferry in 1784 and a year later the Royal Irish Mail's London–Holyhead coaches stopped here. The old city gates were knocked down and the present Eastgate, Northgate, Bridgegate and Watergate archways were built in Classical style to allow easier access.

The satirical John Swift, author of Gulliver's Travels, did not appreciate the coach ride - *'When soon by every hillock rut and stone, In each other's faces by turns were thrown...*

Sweet company! Next time I do protest, Sir, I'd rather walk to Dublin ere I'd ride to Chester' – or the city's clergy whom he invited to dinner but had to dine alone – *'Rotten without and mouldering within, This place and its clergy are nearly akin'* – he scratched on a window pane in the inn where he ate.

His view was not shared by the Cheshire gentlemen who had houses in the city or the biographer James Boswell, who announced that, *'Chester pleases my fancy more than any town I ever saw.'*

Sign at the Pied Bull *GE*

Go to page 68

Bear and Billet *At the foot of Lower Bridge Street this pub was the site of a town house of the Talbots, sergeants of the Bridgegate, rebuilt as a tavern after the Civil War. Look for the upper granary doors and some of the 1620 windows it had a century ago.*

Oddfellows Hall *This Neo-Classical mansion in Lower Bridge Street was built in 1664 and probably altered for John Williams, Attorney-General of Denbighshire in the early 18th century.*

Dutch Houses *near the top of Bridge Street West. Built to a Dutch design, it was re-fronted in the 20th century.*

Bishop Lloyd's *Palace has acquired this grander name since it became the headquarters of Chester Civic Trust. The western half of the house was built for George Lloyd, Bishop of Chester in 1615. His earlier position as Bishop of Sodor and Man (Isle of Man) accounts for the three Legs of Man which also gave its name to the former pub next door. Horses heads are from his family's arms. These and other carvings of biblical scenes can be admired in Watergate Street.*

Bear and Billet   GE

Pied Bull *See Alehouses.*

Pied Bull   JH

Go to page 69

Richer families erected their **Georgian** houses by the riverside, on the amphitheatre site, and west towards the city walls, while the Cathedral authorities built their own in Abbey Square on the foundations of the former abbey brewery and bakehouse. An Improvement Act in 1761 forbade the dumping of '*Ashes, Rubbish, Soil, Timber, Bricks, Stone, Slate, Coals, Dirt, Dung, Filth, Casks and Tubs'* in the city streets and, although gas lights lit these slightly cleaner highways by 1818, ladies with long dresses regularly used sedan chairs to go to social events. Boswell recorded that the city was '*the winter residence of a great many genteel families. It has a Theatre Royal and a very elegant Assembly Room, I never found myself as well received anywhere'.*

The Theatre Royal was originally St Nicholas' Chapel(1280), then St Oswald's (1488-1539), the King's School, the Common Hall(1545), the Wool Hall, the playhouse, the Theatre Royal (1775), the Music Hall(1854), Charles Dickens read here in 1867, the Music Hall Cinema – the oldest building in the world to be used as a cinema(1921-1961), Liptons - the first supermarket inside the City Walls, Fosters, Reject and currently Superdrug.

Chester Castle was almost totally rebuilt in Classical style by Thomas Harrison. The Bluecoat School was enlarged, a Blue Girls' School opened, and the Infirmary led the way in modern practice. The first sod of the Chester Canal was cut to the sound of church bells and a 21 gun salute. Although, at first, the canal suffered from its lack of connection to the main canal systems, by 1805 it linked with the Ellesmere Canal and a link to the Mersey ensured its survival.

The **minstrels** held their last service in St John's Church. A Mr Folliot complained to the newspaper that the city waits played 'till 2 am and destroyed his sleep. (He would not have appreciated today's student nightclubs.) No doubt the waits were trying to get some tips from some of the richer folk who visited public and charity society balls which often had hundreds of invitees. The Exchange had become too small for these events, so the social classes moved to the grand Booth Mansion on Watergate Street. The city supported concerts, dancing and lectures on all subjects even in the summer months. The Chester Summer Music Festival was launched in 1786; the Dee Regatta to 10,000 onlookers in 1814.

Go to page 70

Georgian houses *King Street, Lower Bridge Street, Stanley Place and Nicholas Street have fine examples of Georgian houses in the city. A **Georgian Room** can be seen at the **Grosvenor Museum**.*

minstrels *When buskers were banned in Elizabethan times Chester minstrels, licensed by the Dutton family, were still allowed. This and the story of how this came about is unique. Apparently when Rhuddlan Castle was being besieged in 1198, help came from Chester in the form of minstrels and players who were here for the Midsummer Fair. The constable marched them all into Wales where, at the sight of this large 'army', the Welsh fled. Thereafter, minstrels were licensed by the constable to come to Chester and this right devolved to his steward, John de Dutton. The last minstrels were licensed in 1756 but buskers (not beggars) are still welcome in the city streets.*

Chester Chronicle *Today there are three Chester papers, the Chester Chronicle, The Leader and the Standard (free).*

Grosvenor *Several times in history the head of the Grosvenor Family, now the 7th Duke of Westminster, has been listed as Britain's richest man. With property in Chester, the Eaton Estate four miles upriver, and properties around Belgrave & Mayfair in London it is easy to see why. On the second duke of Westminster's death, in 1853, £19 million was paid in death duties. During the 20th century the fourth duke suffered a shrapnel wound in the war. This was deemed to have caused his death 20 years later so duties were not levied!*

A judgement supported by King Richard II took away the Grosvenor's claimed right to hold the arms azure a bend or (gold band diagonal across blue) and they took on arms linking them with the Cheshire azure a garb or (blue with a gold sheaf). The result was never forgotten though, and in the 19th century the first duke named his racehorse Bend Or and his grandson took on the nickname Bendor. Sir Richard Grosvenor had been made the first baronet in the 17th century, then Hugh Lupus (named after Chester's first earl) became the first duke in the mid-nineteenth century. The family are friends with the Earl of Chester, Prince Charles; occasionally a gold unnumbered Rolls Royce calls in at Eaton.

69

Go to page 71

Shortly afterwards a tourist guide was published, 'The Stranger in Chester' had *'an accurate sketch of local history and a chronological arrangement of the most interesting events... from the most authentic sources',* much like this book.

A public library was started, bull baiting at the Cross abolished but the local cockfighting pit, attended by gentry had a new roof in 1825. Opposite the Exchange was a coffee house where people could relax (Handel drank coffee there) or read a newspaper. Chester had its own Weekly Journal in 1720, and two papers by 1775 – the **Chester Chronicle** is still published.

Politics were heavily influenced by the **Grosvenor** family who helped pay to widen Northgate Street for access in 1781.

The stone built Pentice (town hall) which had replaced the earlier wooden structure was removed in 1803. This drawing is in Lowe's silver shop, Bridge Street East Row, where they moved from their Pentice shop

 Go to page 72

**Sicilian marble
statue of the
Second Marquis
of Westminster in
Grosvenor Park** *GE*

From 1679 to 1868 one of the Grosvenors usually served as the city's MPs. Gladstone called Hugh Lupus a selfish aristocrat when he refused to support the Reform Bill of 1866, but Hugh went on to support a similar bill for the following government and other bills to improve the lot of the poorer classes while supporting hospitals and charities.

The grand mansion at Eaton has been completely rebuilt three times: a gothic hall with spires that took 12 years to build was started in 1870 but, all except the chapel, was replaced by a new hall in the 1960s. **The grounds are open to the public three times a year on Bank Holidays.**

Westminster Coach Works in Northgate Street, later the library *GE*

Go to page 73

Three years later they spent £15,000 in 90 alehouses to ensure election to Parliament. The following year the Royal Hotel (now Chester Grosvenor) was rebuilt with large assembly rooms and a coffee lounge. In 1808 a Christmas pie given by Earl Grosvenor for the Exchange banquet weighed 69 kilos.

Unfortunately the fire regulations did little to stop fires and in 1853 the police/fireman refused to do both jobs as the work was *'too onerous'*. Nine years later the Exchange burnt down. The City of Chester Fire Brigade was formed the following year.

VICTORIAN CREATIONS

A major change to Chester streets took place in 1832 when Princess Victoria opened the Grosvenor Bridge. A new road, Grosvenor Street, led into the city cutting diagonally across the existing road pattern and resulting in the demolition of **St Bridget's Church.** At the other end of the city, the new railway came in 1840. The **General Station** with its 307 metre Italianate frontage opened eight years later. It was soon decided that another road had to be built to the city so, in 1866, City Road was built leading to Foregate Street. Horsedrawn **trams** in crimson-lake and cream livery soon followed. The station clock was moved off centre so it could be seen approaching the station up the new road.

A new phase of building took place. Curzon Park, across the river from the Roodee became a rich suburb after Lord Curzon built a house for his mistress there, complete with an upper balcony above the roof where the races could be watched. Queen's Park and a private suspension bridge (later replaced with a public one) linking it to the city was built upriver, above Handbridge.

In the city Gothic buildings can be seen at the Paparazzi Restaurant beside the Grosvenor Museum, **Browns of Chester** and the **Town Hall.** Chester's Victorian **black and white** revival frontages and buildings can be found on most city centre streets. Both God's Providence House and Bishop's Lloyd's Palace in Watergate Street had new frontages, as did the Art Gallery at 61 Bridge Street. **Shoemakers' Row** at the foot of Northgate Street, the Cross Buildings, and most of St Werburgh Street were rebuilt. Superb brick, stone and terracotta buildings include Queen's

Go to page 74

St Bridget's Church   *Gravestones from the demolished church can still be seen on the Grosvenor Roundabout by the Castle.*

General Station   *Thomas Brassey (see his bust in the Cathedral or the plaque at the station) built this grand statement to Chester's Victorian importance, to a plan by Francis Thomson. By 1850 there were six railway companies operating from here.*

***Old Bank Buildings**   JH*

trams   *One-horse cars, with bells to warn pedestrians, ran through the city streets on rails by 1879. In the 20th century, electric open-top vehicles were brought in and continued until 1930 when buses replaced them.*

73

Go to page 75

School, the bank beside the Eastgate, the Grosvenor Museum, houses in Bath Street and the whole east side of Grosvenor Park Road, not forgetting the Bull & Stirrup, beyond the Northgate.

On the outskirts of the city, market gardens and seed producers flourished on the fields in Sealand, recovered from the Dee when it was canalised. Although there were several small manufacturers around the town at the beginning of the Victorian era they soon declined while industries within the City Walls were discouraged, or could not find large enough sites. In fact, Chester almost missed out on the Industrial Revolution. Steamworks and some **leadworks** grew along the canal but other works were across the river in Saltney. The result was that some of the poorer citizens were living in slums and over-populated courts. The only work available for them was in service or as labourers for low wages and long hours. In one of the first attempts at slum clearance, C T Parker, agent for the Grosvenors, had John Douglas build a three storey tenement with separate flats for retired Eaton Estate workers in Foregate Street.

Chester's popularity was still because of its ancient and county town beginnings and its continuing retail trade: Browns became known as 'the Harrods of the North'. The city's port and linen trade were losing out to Liverpool. Tourism began to be a major input to the city, and the new teacher's training college, opened by Gladstone in 1842, gave the city an educational importance. The college became Chester University.

When American author Henry James visited in 1872 he found himself *'strolling and restrolling along the ancient wall – so perfect in its antiquity'*. He went on to realise that *'starting at any point, an hour's stroll will bring you back' (see Walk the Walls). 'If the picturesque be measured by its hostility to our modern notion of convenience'*, he stated, *Chester is possibly the most romantic city in the world.'*

THE 20TH CENTURY

With the city's change to electricity on DC power, a new light and bright Edwardian Row, actually an arcade, was built for the Duke of Westminster through the existing shops at first storey level. However, he had not recognised the citizens' pride so that the front of the building decorated in white tile was almost

Go to page 76

Stanley Palace, Watergate Street GE

Browns of Chester *This gothic frontage can be seen on* **Eastgate Street South**. *In 1929 the shop's first floor had a 'model electric home' described as an improvement on the model home at the Wembley exhibition. Inside could be found such labour-saving items as an electric toaster, electric percolator, electric bed warmer, electric massage set, and electric curling irons. As if this wasn't enough 'the envy of housewives' was the electric cooker, electric washing machines and the 'indispensible (sic) electric iron'.*

Statue of King
Charles I at 61 Bridge
Street Row East GE

black and white revival *Architects John Douglas, T M Lockwood and his son WM Lockwood were instrumental in designing many of the Victorian facades and buildings now seen in Chester. Look for the Art Gallery in* **Bridge Street Row East** *with its statue of King Charles I.*

Shoemakers' Row *The original row on* **Northgate Street West** *was medieval and similar to those opposite except that some of its undercrofts or cellars only had very low doors for entrances. Above, on the first floor gallery shoes and boots hung from the ceiling as advertisements. Part of the Row was demolished for the Commercial Coffee Rooms in 1808, later the Commercial Newsroom. The rest was replaced to designs by John Douglas and James Strong (see pages 10 and 57).*

Go to page 77

immediately changed to black and white timbering after a public outcry, although the lower part and the inside were left untouched. Tramways were electrified and extended. In 1913, a hydro-electric station supplemented existing power.

During World War I both soldiers and German prisoners came to Chester. With higher wages after the war, cinemas, such as the **Odeon** and the Regal, and dance halls brought enjoyment to thousands of Cestrians.

Americans stationed here in the Second World War might also find enjoyment at the **King's Arms Kitchen** pub. The 'Mayor's Chair' in the mock Mayor's Parlour was used by locals as a source of free drinks when it was explained to the soldier invited to sit there that it was the custom that anyone in the chair had to buy a round of beer. *(It is now in the Grosvenor Museum.)*

Apart from the ever-present danger of firebombs, the city was virtually untouched by bombers due to its lack of heavy industry although many of its citizens had joined the **Cheshire Regiment** fighting in Europe and never returned.

In 1948 the earl of Chester, Prince Charles, was born. He was given freedom of the city in 1973. Queen Elizabeth visited Chester Races in 1966. In 1992 she visited again to create Chester's first Lord Mayor (Sue Proctor).

THE AGE OF THE AUTOMOBILE

As a retailing city serving a wide country area of Cheshire and North Wales, it is easy to see why, with the growth of the car and the later decline and closure of parts of the railway system, Chester streets became a logjam of traffic by the 1930s; the ancient city streets could not cope. One answer, to divert cars along Pepper Street through a newly built Newgate, was immediately compromised by the discovery of the amphitheatre – the road had to go around it. This became part of the inner ring-road: by 1972 a mass of Georgian houses had been torn down, flyovers built and the Walls cut through to divert traffic around the city. Architecturally the city suffered in the latter half of the 20th century. The eastern side of the ring-road along Nicholas Street was filled with blank-walled buildings, and a similar blank wall replaced the earlier market.

Go to page 78

leadworks   *Go east **along the canal** for less than a mile to see the world's last Lead Shot Tower, used in the Napoleonic wars to make high-quality shot for British soldiers. Molten metal was dropped through the air to cool, before it landed in water below. The lead works was only closed at the end of the 20th century.*

Odeon   More than half the population visited cinemas once a week by the 1940s. This Art Deco cinema is a listed building and has been converted into Storyhouse with the addition of a theatre.

A Celebration of Chester by Stephen Broadbent

King's Arms Kitchen   *Now in the Grosvenor Museum.*

Cheshire Regiment   *The Garden of Remembrance is in the Cathedral grounds. See also Museums.*

Chester Castle 1815

Tower hamlets were built in Newtown. Ugly concrete buildings at Salmon Leap, beyond the weir, replaced a tobacco mill although its unusual pink frontage today makes it strangely acceptable. Two concrete monstrosities, the concrete Rows in Watergate Street and St Martin's Gate (a bridge over the inner ring-road), amazingly won design awards when they were built. There was a return to brick and stone in the Magistrates Court of 1995 – although it could be mistaken for a Chinese Restaurant. An unusual design was Centurion House in Northgate Street with its faceted dark glass.

It was not until 1981 that the city streets began to be reclaimed for pedestrians. This change of use now includes the main central streets and it is almost impossible to imagine how the shoppers would have fitted in without it. Pedestrianisation of the city centre has resulted in cleaner, healthier streets and a more pleasant environment for residents and tourists alike. Lessons might have been learnt from the brash 1960s: an interesting design for the HQ building opposite the Castle is mostly sandstone and glass replacing a concrete police headquarters, but two new glaring white buildings along the inner ring-road outside the Northgate are possibly the ugliest built in half a century. New buildings should fit in or excel in the cityscape, while not obscuring those already here.

The city's protectionism from Roman beginnings, through medieval trades, Georgian opulence, and the reluctance of Victorians to have industry within the walls have all resulted in a place where people still want to work, live and visit. It is Chester's fortune that the city's past is the very thing that has ensured its future. At present, at least, the green belt and open spaces that we all need have kept the city linked to the countryside that supports it. If you are a visitor to our city, come again and see more.

Moored up for the night in Chester Canal basin GE

CHESTER CATHEDRAL

St John the Baptist Church was the original Saxon Minster then the Norman Cathedral. Today's Cathedral is on the site of St Werburgh's Abbey. In the early tenth century, the remains of St Werburgh were brought to the city from Staffordshire ostensibly to protect the holy relics from the marauding Danes, but probably also as a statement of intent to make Chester the most important fortified city in the north of the Mercian kingdom, by having one of the Mercian royal family buried here. The church was rededicated to St Werburgh while St Peter's was moved to its present position. A stained glass window in the refectory tells the story of how, at the attack of King Gruffydd of Wales, her relics were carried to the top of the city walls and 'struck the king blind' so that he retreated.

The first Norman earl, Hugh founded St Werbugh's Abbey for Benedictine monks in 1092. Most of the abbey was built in just over a century. Then the monks started to knock down the abbey church and rebuild it. This amazing building programme lasted a total of 435 years. Norman building work can still be seen in the Baptistry, the North Transept and the shop and reception area.

St Werburgh's Shrine c1310 was originally decorated with 34 Mercian princes and princesses. Werburgh, the daughter of Wulfere, King of Mercia (658-675), as a nun, was given control of all the Mercian nunneries. (Look also, for the little dog carving.)

A carved misericord in the quire shows three scenes from the legend of St Werburgh. In the late 14th century woodcarvers came from Lincoln to build the tabernacled stalls. Forty-three medieval scenes remain under the seats. Most of the bench ends from the period have survived. Look for the elephant, an animal obviously unknown to the carver, with horses' hooves; a pelican, symbol of piety, restores its young with blood from its own breast.

Misericord of St Werburgh's miracle

(For a full catalogue and photographs of the medieval misericords see 'Medieval Imagination in Chester Cathedrals'.)

Chester Imp Like Lincoln, Chester has its own imp. A stone carving on the north balcony of the nave is said to represent the Devil, bound hands and feet. It was apparently put there to frighten off the Devil if he should try to look through the window to see the holy sacrament.

Chester Imp   photo: S Atkinson

It is possible that this Devil from the north is based on the Norse god Loki who was bound for his crimes and appears in other northern Christian carvings notably the Gosforth Cross.

The abbey became rich with gifts of land, and also received the tolls of the stalls set up before the abbey gate on Saint John the Baptist's Day. However, when Bishop Norbury visited in the early 14th century he found that the abbot had increasing debts and too many personal servants. The abbot's sins included eating meat in his quarters on fish days and hunting with greyhounds. By the 16th century the wealth of the abbeys and Roman Catholic Church was coveted by Henry VIII who closed them down, sold their lands and pocketed the proceeds while setting himself and the future Crown of England as the Divine head of the new English Catholic Church.

However, unlike many religious houses and monasteries, the abbey was converted into the **Cathedral of Christ and the Blessed Virgin Mary**, with the former abbot becoming the new dean. Without the former riches, little outer building work was done for centuries, so the building fell into disrepair.

Green Man There are 16 images of the Green Man in the Cathedral, including on a stone boss near the Visitor entrance, on a bench end and on a misericord.

Spires and gargoyles are the results of major restoration work of the Cathedral carried out mainly in the 19th century. Building a new song school above the Monk's Parlour started in 2002.

Green Man in the cloister roof   GE

CATHEDRAL PLAN

Saint Oswald's Church: A part of the Saxon minster had been the parish church. In the 13th century ot was probably in the south aisle of the nave. by 1488, St Nicholas' Chapel in St Werburgh Street was rededicated to St Oswald but by 1539 the parishioners had returned to the south transept. The Parish Church of Saint Oswald was later partitioned (1828 - 1880) from the main cathedral. St Oswald's parishioners moved to the new St Thomas Church in Parkgate Road during 1881. The church has recently been rededicated to St Oswald and St Thomas.

The Slype: A slype is a narrow covered passage usually leading to the monks' burial places.

The Nave was paved in 1600 and repaired in 1777. Another new floor was laid in 1997 after an extensive archaeological dig.

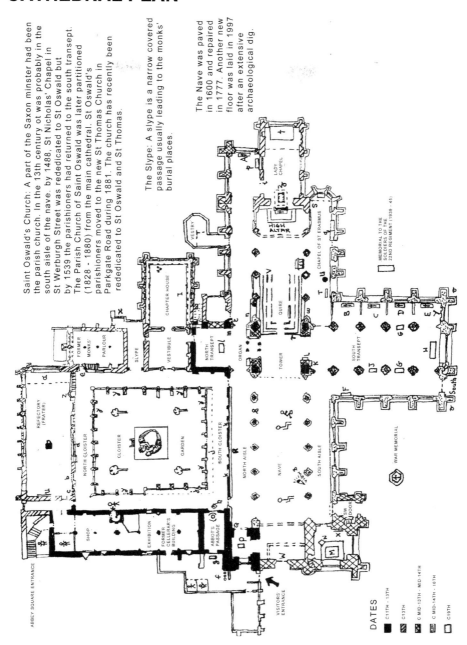

DATES

■	C11TH - 13TH
■	C13TH
▨	C MID-13TH - MID-14TH
▧	C MID-14TH - 16TH
☐	C19TH

Key to Cathedral Plan

A Chapel of St Werburgh (Christian Unity) B St Mary Magdalene Chapel (Children's Chapel) C St Oswald's Chapel D St George's Chapel (Cheshire Reg't since 1912) E St Nicholas' and St Leonard's Chapel (Saints of children and pensioners) F RAF Memorial chapel G Book of Names, Cheshire Regiment H Chester Hearse Cloth I Burial place of the Norman Earls J First Duke of Westminster Memorial K Chester Memorial L Memorial to Thomas Green (Mayor 1565) and his wives. The hands may have been smashed by Puritans after the Civi War M Consistory Court 1636 (The only surviving in England) N Apparitor's Chair O Above is the Chapel of St Anselm (reserved for services) P Font in the Baptistry Q Nine Men's Morris Board carving R Four Mosaics of Old Testament scenes (1883-6) S Thomas Brassey bust T Tomb said to be for Godescallus (Henry V of Aquitaine) U Gurney Radiator once used coke in the boiler V Quire stalls include carved misericords, bench ends and corbels W Stained glass Virgin & Child with six northern saints X St John Ambulance & Red Cross banner 1914-19 Y Sedile (clergy's seat) Z Stone pulpit

a stained glass of St Werburgh and her relations includes casket repelling Welsh invaders and Ethelred resigning Crown on Werburgh's advice b Early English c 1200 door to Refectory c Recessed cupboards d Monk's lavatorium (wash place) e Stairs to dorter (monks' dormitory) Conversion to purpose-built Song School f Roof bosses include a Green Man g Monks' vestment cupboard h Later column blocks early doorway i Overhead bosses: Holy Trinity, Our Lady & Child, St Thomas Beckett's martyrdom j Carols (monk's study places) k Burial places of early abbots l Memorial to Bishop (1672-86) John Pearson m Caterpillar web picture from Tyrol n Remains of Norman quire o Carved heads including Gladstone & Disraeli p Monument of Bishop (1848-65) Graham q Ranulph Higden's tomb and two others r Quire screen (Gilbert Scott 1876) s Chester Imp on the balcony t Remains of fireplace u C16th Cartoon tapestry v Stained-glass of earls and King Henry VIII w Portions of old organ screen x Stained-glass Ranulph Higden y Stained-glass saints and apostles (1921-27) z St Werburgh Shrine (restored 1888)

RIVERSIDE GROVES

Chester's Old Dee Bridge, ancient weir, pedestrian suspension bridge, boats, artists' stalls, swans and ducks – just a few things to see if you stroll along the riverside, sit under the lime trees by the bandstand, (bands on summer Sundays, some Saturdays and Bank Holidays) or outside a cafe or pub beside the Dee.

There are boat cruises to take, paddle boats, rowing boats and motor boats to hire on the River Dee.

The **Old Dee Bridge**

was recorded in the Domesday Book of 1086 and there was almost certainly a bridge here in Roman times. The Mayor's book for 1390 records that *'no person having a cart with iron-bound wheels shall permit it to cross Dee Bridge on forfeit of the cart and 6s8d to the king'* but technology couldn't be held back so when, in 1533, Henry ap Res allowed carts to cross he was pardoned by the mayor. In 1574 defences included *'in the middle thereof a gate of lern (iron) which in the night was taken up'.*

Toll fees, abolished in 1885, included 9d for a carriage, 2d for a saddle horse. The Coroners' accounts include the final result of some pedestrians who waded across to save paying the toll and were swept away.

The bridge was widened in 1826 but the stonework on the downstream side kept its medieval refuges, built above the cutwaters to protect pedestrians from herds of animals crossing.

Britain's oldest recorded **weir** was built across the river to supply water power for the Dee Mills. Over the centuries mills have produced everything from flour and oatmeal to snuff and needlepoints. Canoeists regularly use the **salmon steps** for white water practice while cormorants, swans and a variety of gulls and ducks rest on the stonework which was raised in 1913 for the **hydroelectric station** built to supplement the city's power.

The iron **'YMCA'** gate led to a former hostel there, now offices but formerly the Georgian house of the Bishop of Chester.

The large building opposite, built in the style of a Roman temple is the modern addition to what were the plain brick buildings of the **Western Command HQ**, described by Pevsner in Buildings of England as a 'nonentity'.

The **bandstand** was built for £350; the mounted band of the Royal Artillery was the first band to play here on 17th May 1913.

The Groves were laid out with lime trees in 1725 paid for by Charles Croughton, swordbearer of the city; and the western end by Alderman Brown of Browns of Chester in the 1880's. The rough frontage at the eastern end was replaced a century later with a brick floored walkway, although the houseowners maintain their riparian rights with private landing stages.

Rock House GE

A Chester legend tells how King Harold, wounded in one eye at the Battle of Hastings, found refuge here in the original **Anchorite Cell** of St John the Baptist Church. The present building on its rock base dates from the mid-14th century and was later converted into the two-storey private house that is there today.

Queen's Park Suspension Bridge replaced an earlier private bridge in 1923. Shields of the city's seven Norman earls decorate its towers. However, the dangerous game of jumping from it to the river below caused a fatal accident in 2002.

Over the years the strong currents have resulted in many fatalities even to strong swimmers. At the end of the 19th century there was a floating bath house here with canvas sides but the advent of indoor warmer baths made it uneconomic.

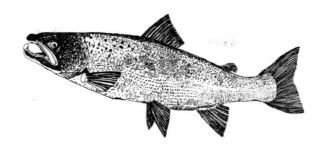

Salmon *GE*

Across the bridge upriver is an open space known as **The Meadows** open for walking or picnicking. This was also known as **Earls Eyes** in an Elizabethan sale document and presumably named after the islands formed in flood on the earl's land here.

Queen's Park Suspension Bridge *JH*

ALEHOUSES

Over 500 names have been recorded for Chester public houses, although only 182 have existed at one time. Names such as the Sun, Moon, and Angel have gone together with the Horse & Bags, Dairy Maid, Brewer's Dray, Corkcutters' Arms, and the Blackamoor's Head which reflect their time period, although the Cross Keys' name has moved from the Cathedral to Lower Bridge Street.

The Blue Bell is now a restaurant. The signed date just refers to its licensing by an Act of Parliament, the pub probably dates to the 14th century with parts dating back to the 11th. GE

The Liverpool Arms by the Northgate has changed its name several times. As the Loggerheads Tavern it once had a sign with a picture of two clowns and the motto, *'We Three Loggerheads'* – the viewer being the third. It has also been the Bull & Dog and Dog & Partridge.

The mistake, while painting the name of the Malbororough Arms in St John Street has been kept on its new sign. Leche House (Sofa Workshop) in Watergate Street Row South was the Hand & Snake. Look inside to see why.

Laws against serving bad beer are recorded in Chester from before 1066. The brewer could be put in the 'cucking stool' or fined 4 shillings. In 1494, Justices of the Peace were able to *'put away common ale selling where they should think convenient'*. Prices were strictly controlled; in 1590 the City Assembly ordered that *'ale to be no more than a penny a quart and it to be full'*. Those were the days!

Even those who served the beer were regulated *'...eny women being betwene fourteen and forty years of age"* were barred, from 1540, to prevent *'dishonest report of this citie'*. The council also found a free way to light the streets. From 1503 during winter *'all innkeepers as well that have sygnez as they that have no sygnez shall have hanging at ther dore a lantorne with a candyll bryning in it'*. At 9pm, after the curfew bell was rung, the lights went out and, supposedly, everyone went home.

Some of the oldest pubs still exist. The Blue Bell was just the Bell in 1399, the Pied Bull was serving beer by 1571 and some say they can still feel the presence of John Davies, who, in 1690, *'casually fell down a pair of stairs leading to the Sellar belonging to the Pide Bull inn and with a knife in his hand... and dyed'*.

Bulls, cows and horses were popular names around the cattle market thus 'The Bull and Stirrup' now a Wetherspoons with many real ales. JH

Gone are the breweries such as Bents with its XXX Ale, and the Northgate Brewery which drew its water from deep within the city's bedrock, but a new microbrewery is at the Pied Bull.

There are many licensed premises in the city, including hotels open to non-residents, licensed restaurants, wine bars, clubs and entertainment venues. The alehouses listed below are within the city walls and have cask real ales.

Alexanders Live Rufus Court Northgate Street   Live music, comedy.

Albion Albion Street   World War I memorabilia.

Architect   Commemorating Thomas Harrison in his former Georgian house on Nicholas Street.

Bear & Billet Lower Bridge Street   Rebuilt after the Civil War, drink in one of the city's finest.

Old Boot Inn   Built in the Civil War, look for the musket ball inside as well as the horsetraders' bench. Low priced beer.

Brewery Tap Lower Bridge Street   Formerly Gamul House where King Charles I ate dinner with the mayor.

The Church Bar Newgate Street   In a superbly restored church.

The Coach Northgate Street   Food & drink near Storyhouse.

Cross Keys Lower Bridge Street   Nineteenth century detail and wood panelling.

Custom House Inn Watergate Street   Pay your customs on beer here opposite the Old Custom House.

Falcon Bridge Street   A row is enclosed in this medieval townhouse. The pub was a tea-totallers' cocoa house at the end of the 19th century. Low priced beer.

Golden Eagle Castle Street Pub site used from 1622, jukebox

Liverpool Arms Northgate Street   Gay friendly pub.

Ye Olde King's Head 17th Century Tudor-style pub with rooms allegedly featuring timber recovered from one of Lord Nelson's sunken ships.

Music Hall Tap St Werburgh Street   New bar 2018.

Pied Bull Northgate Street Chester's oldest remaining former coaching inn, Tudor staircase, microbrewery.

Plumbers' Arms Newgate Street Craft beers, live entertainment.

Red Lion Northgate Street   Built around 1600, Sky sports.

Shropshire Arms Northgate Street   Get beer here before the theatre or cinema.

Victoria Watergate Street Row North   An old pub on the Rows.

Other pubs: go outside the city walls and the list becomes greater: there are pubs in Frodsham Street, Brook Street, City Road, Handbridge, Garden Quarter and Hoole. Walk out along the canal to Christleton and Waverton to find even more.

'A mere passage' St Peter's Churchyard JH

In November 1636, complaint was made that 'the way is used thorow the Church and Churchyard to the said three doors going to the said three houses next adjoining to drink Wyne, beer and ale upon Sundays, holidayes and other days. And divers persons go thorowe the said churchyard to the said severall tap houses at there (sic) pleasure to drink makinge the Churchyard a mere passage...' They still do!

BOOKS on Chester and North Wales from Gordon
Emery   Order at Visitor Information, Waterstones, Beatons Books or online: www.gordonemery.co.uk (free post UK)

Curious Chester, Portrait of an English city over 2000 years
Gordon Emery £15.95

Chester Inside Out, A walk around the ancient walled city
Gordon Emery £7.95

Medieval Imagination in Chester Cathedral, Myth, Misericords, Miracles, Monsters, Mystery Plays, Midsummer Watch and the Green Man
Gordon Emery £7.95

Chester Walls, Discover the Roman and Medieval Walls
(included in this guide)   *Gordon Emery £2.50*

Roman Chester DEVA, Discover Chester's Ancient Ruins
Gordon Emery & Roy Wilding £2.95

Postcard Map of Chester, Use the map, send the postcards
Jay Hurst & Gordon Emery £1,50

Miller of Dee, The Story of Chester Mills and Millers, their Trades and Wares, the Weir, the Water Engine and the Salmon *Roy Wilding £9.99*

Boom of the Bitterbump, The Folk-history of Cheshire's Wildlife
Roger Stephens £11.95

Hidden Highways of Cheshire, Ten Circular Walks exploring Roman Roads, Salter's Ways, Lost Lanes, Medieval Roads *R J Dutton £9.99*

Hidden Highways of North Wales, Ten Circular Walks exploring Roman Roads, Drovers' Ways, Packhorse Trails, Ancient Tracks, and Lost Lanes – and a Ghost Story *R J Dutton £9.99*

Underground Clywd, The Armchair Explorers' Guide; A pictorial expedition into the nether regions of Northeast Wales *Cris Ebbs £9.99*

Curious Clwyd, A Photographic Album of Oddities from Northeast Wales
Gordon Emery £11.95

Curious Clwyd, A Second Photographic Album of Oddities from N Wales
Gordon Emery £11.95

Guide to the Maelor Way Grindley Brook to Chirk *Gordon Emery £3.95*

Daywalks, Vale of Llangollen *Gordon Emery & John Roberts £2.95*

Walks (in Clwyd) see titles online *Gordon Emery booklets £1.50 each*

Limited edition of 50 numbered A3 mounted prints of misericords (see p 79) from Chester Cathedral **Chester Art Centre** *or* **email from website** *£50 each print*